MW00442830

The Scrum Princess

by Kyle and Demi Aretae

Illustrations by Mike Motz

Kyle Dedication:
To Misti, who started the metaphor

To Laura and Tom, who encouraged
my exuberant storytelling

And to my wife, Demetria,
who made the book happen.

Demi Dedication:
To Kyle, who continues to inspire me.

The Scrum Princess
© 2016 Kyle and Demi Aretae. All Rights reserved.

No part of this publication may be reproduced or transmitted in any
form or by any means, electronic, mechanical, including photocopy,
recording, or any information storage and retrieval system, without
permission in writing from the author.

Printed in the United States of America

The Scrum Princess

Once upon a time in a land far, far away lived a Princess who had lots of gold.

While riding around in her rickety carriage one day, the Princess made a big decision.

"I am going to use my gold to make my kingdom the most beautiful place in the world. Everyone will want to come and live here, and all of the people will be happy.

She told her servants to call the Wizard, Master Scrum.

"Master Scrum," the Princess said, "I want a better carriage. I want a fence around the castle. I want a well. I want the roof on the castle repaired, and I want a pet hippopotamus to frolic in the pasture. I want a supply of firewood for three months."

And on and on and on...

Master Scrum assured the Princess that he could help her to get the most important things that she wanted, but that trying to do everything all at once would make everything go slower. "We need to figure out what is most important, so we can do that first."

As princesses are wont to do, she assured him that *everything* was top priority.

Master Scrum carefully pointed out that doing one thing first would require some other things to not be first.

After a small tantrum, she said, "Fine... we'll try it your way."

Master Scrum went into the town and spoke to the peasants.

"Friends, peasants, coworkers," he said, "The Princess has a pile of gold. She wants to spend it to make her kingdom the best place in all the world. Shall we form a team and become well paid by doing her work? I can help us work together well. Who will join me?"

The next morning, Master Scrum returned to the Princess with a team of four workers: a Painter, a Lumberjack, a Tailor, and a Miner. They gathered in the throne room to talk about the work that the Princess had for them to do.

The Princess gave Master Scrum her list. "This is the list of things I want. Start now."

Master Scrum interjected, "Princess, to gain the most value from your gold, you must permit me to do this somewhat differently than what you are accustomed to."

The Princess agreed to listen to Master Scrum's magical ways but warned him, "There will be dire consequences if the work is not accomplished quickly."

Master Scrum began with the Ceremony of Sizing. This ceremony exists to ensure serious engagement with the work. Many workers won't seriously think about work until they're asked to do something with it.

Master Scrum started the ceremony. "We need to discover how much work the Princess's top priorities will take, so that she can do real cost-benefit analyses on which to do first. For her to prioritize without knowing something about the cost would be irresponsible. Let us size the stories in relation to each other."

Suppose we start by comparing two stories. Which one is harder, and which will be done quicker between these two:

First story: The Princess wants to have a fence around the pasture so that her cows stop wandering off.

Second story: The Princess wants a well near the castle so she doesn't have to wait for a river trip to get fresh water.

After much deliberation and questioning of the Princess, the team ordered the stories from easiest to hardest.

The team shared their findings with the princess:

"Fixing the carriage is easiest. We can do that fast."

"The Hippopotamus will take almost forever. Africa is far away."

"I WANT MY HIPPO!" screamed the Princess.

Master Scrum intervened. "Princess, you may specify in what order your wishes are fulfilled, but you may not change how far away Africa is.

"Please let us proceed to the next ceremony: the Ceremony of Queuing. This ceremony exists to direct the team's focus."

"Princess, now that you know how difficult each item is, please confer with the court and place them in order. What should your team focus their efforts on first?"

The Princess gathered her court. The Jester wanted to play with the hippo in the pasture. The Court Magician thought that repairing the roof should be first because it would improve the overall image of the kingdom. The Royal Vizier just wanted to ensure that someone was counting the costs of all of these improvements. Every member of her court was able to make suggestions. Even the King had an opinion. The Princess listened to all of them, made her list, and presented it to Master Scrum.

"First I want the fence. Then I want the roof fixed. Then I want the carriage fixed. The well is next, and the hippo is after that. Now GET GOING!"

Master Scrum addressed the team, "We have now completed the Ceremonies of Sizing and Queuing. We have one more ceremony before we begin work."

Master Scrum proclaimed, "Team, the Princess has decided that fence building is the most important activity. Let us begin the Ceremony of Clarification. This ceremony exists to create a shared understanding of the broader details of the work."

The team asked the Princess many questions. Should it be a wood fence, a metal fence, or stone? How tall should it be? Where would the fence go? Is the fence decorative, or does it have a goal? Does the fence need to keep something in or out? How far apart should the posts be?

After some deliberation, the team ended up with a pretty good shared understanding of the goal. Some of the questions helped the Princess get a better idea of what she wanted.

The team discussed the discrete tasks necessary to build the fence. They clarified some details with the Princess. They estimated how long each task would take in half-day increments.

In the afternoon, Master Scrum introduced the Standing Circle Ceremony to help the team coordinate quickly and learn to share responsibility.

Master Scrum taught the workers to coordinate their plans efficiently, without interrupting each other.

Three team members prepared to apply their specialty to the project, but the Tailor's expertise was unnecessary in fence building.

"I will go with the Lumberjack and chop trees," the Tailor said. "By working together I can learn something and we will work faster together."

I will BEGIN by chopping TREES TODAY

I will dig POST-HOLES FOR THE FENCES TODAY

I will GO FIND PIGMENTS FOR MY PAINT

They all went off and worked their selected tasks for the day. Even with Scrum, doing the work is the most important part of getting things done.

The next morning, Master Scrum again called the daily Standing Circle Ceremony.

The Lumberjack reported that he and the tailor chopped four trees yesterday, and they expected to chop six more today.

The Artist reported that she completed collecting pigments yesterday, and she planned to mix the pigments today.

The Miner shared that he dug five holes, but then a dragon came. The Miner refused to go back into the field until the dragon was gone.

The rest of the team went about their business. The Miner joined the Artist to help with her paints.

Master Scrum went looking for someone to deal with the dragon. After several draconic misadventures with a witch, a shepherd, and a dragon removal engineer, Master Scrum found Sir Dragonslayer. And after bit of negotiation, Sir Dragonslayer went out to remove the dragon.

The next morning, Master Scrum called the Standing Circle Ceremony to order.

Sir Dragonslayer announced the slaying of the dragon. And there was much rejoicing.

The workers all returned to their tasks. The Miner got back to digging, and the rest of the two weeks proceeded without further impediments.

At the end of two weeks, the fence was complete and purple.

Master Scrum met with the Princess and reported that the fence was done. They looked it over together, and the Princess learned everything about the fence.

It was three feet tall. It was made of solid pine. The post caps were the things most likely to wear, and they were easily replaceable. It could handle four full-grown cows leaning on it at the same time without collapsing. It matched her favorite dress.

Master Scrum then asked the Princess to invite everyone to the Show and Tell Ceremony. The work team, the Princess's team, the King, the Queen, and the king from the next kingdom over all attended the ceremony.

The Princess presented her new fence.

The other royalty made tactful suggestions.

Master Scrum asked the Princess whether the job, as described by the Princess in the first meeting, was done.

She agreed that it was complete, and Master Scrum crossed the fence off the Princess's list.

Master Scrum left the royalty to their party and pulled the team aside.

The final ceremony for each cycle is the Retrospective Ceremony. This ceremony exists to direct attention to and improve the team's effectiveness.

Master Scrum led with the invocation, "We will focus upon things within our control. We will not blame one another."

A short ceremony ensued, focused on (a) current imperfections, (b) current successes, and (c) a single practice to improve for the next cycle. The team concluded that they should do better dragon inspection with their next job. While dragons are smelly and unpleasant, being surprised by dragons is actually dangerous. The Tailor volunteered to ensure that someone on the team read the dragon forecast each day, and to personally stick his head outdoors and smell for smoke.

After a well-deserved weekend of rest for everyone, Master Scrum asked the Princess to look at the list again. And he had questions: Shall we continue working for you? And is the list of priorities in order?

The Princess agreed, and demanded that the work continue. She also updated the list.

And the cycle continued.

Several cycles later, things had gotten much better. The carriage, the roof, and the fence were complete. Then the spare tower got repaired when the Princess's new baby brother came to live with them, and that became top priority.

The well was never built. Instead they built a much cheaper new canal.

After a few months, the Princess forgot all about the hippo. "Oh, that silly idea," she said when she saw it on the list. "Let's throw that away."

The Scrum Team was still together, well-paid and happily continuing to work for the Princess. The townspeople were happy, and the Princess was happy. They hosted a grand celebration, and ambassadors from all over the world come to admire the beautiful new kingdom. Everyone wanted to come and live in the Princess's kingdom, and all her subjects were happy.

And they all lived happily ever after.

The Scrum Princess

Glossary

Scrum: A software project management methodology named after the rugby method of restarting play. The best known of the Agile methodologies.

Agile: A category of software development methodologies focused on building a team and software that respond effectively to change.

Master Scrum (The Scrum Master Role): One of three roles in Scrum, charged with removing impediments which prevent the team from working effectively, and with ensuring the process flows smoothly. The phrase "servant leader" is legally required to be used when discussing this role.

Princess (The Product Owner Role): The person with the responsibility of knowing what needs to get done, explaining it to the team, striking a balance between different stakeholders' competing priorities, and deciding what to do when things change.

The Team (Role): Scrum focuses on the notion that the entire team is responsible for building the product. We avoid saying things like, " Beth is responsible for the code, and Sam is responsible for the tests." The whole team is responsible for the tests **and** the code. A benefit of shared responsibility is that team members never say, "That's not my job."

The Dragon (Impediment): Impediments are a critical part of what is discussed in the standup, and impediment removal is a big part of the Scrum Master's job. On software projects, most impediments will be people and competing priorities (not dragons), but the same principle remains: remove the problem somehow. Our experience suggests that the most effective impediment removal tools are ongoing relationship development and management... with occasional bribery (coffee, chocolate, etc...).

The Work (Stories): Scrum divides work into stories, each specifying who wants what, and why. We introduced this only in passing.

Standing Circle Ceremony (The Daily Scrum Event): A short, focused, daily occurrence that allows the team to coordinate. Specifically built to (a) NOT be a project status meeting, (b) to replace the project status meeting, and (c) finish quickly (5-15 min).

Ceremony of Sizing (Sprint Planning Event): In formal Scrum, this is part of either the Sprint Planning Event, or potentially part of the not formally defined "backlog grooming" or "storytime." While many of us in the industry find sizing and estimation very useful, there are some who we respect who oppose the practice.

Ceremony of Queuing (Sprint Planning Event): In formal Scrum, this is the other part of the Sprint Planning event.

The Sprint (Event): This is the term we use to describe one cycle from Sizing and Queuing to Retrospective. We didn't use this term in our discussion...the main part of the story deals with the events of one sprint, with nods at the fact that sprints continue until the work is done. These days, Scrum calls the sprint an event.

Retrospective Ceremony (Event): Time when the team figures out how to get a little better for the next sprint.

Show and Tell Ceremony (Sprint Review Event): This ceremony asks the question, "Is this what you wanted us to build? Is it *still* what you want?" Building the wrong software is a much bigger problem than building the software wrong.

Princess's List (Product Backlog Artifact): The product owner needs to have some notion of what work is next. The list is prioritized and changeable, and must be written down somewhere.

The Team's Board (Sprint Backlog Artifact): Experienced Agilists often prefer that new teams use a physical board, especially early in the team's life-cycle. Using a physical board is important because it allows the team to make bigger changes to their board more easily, while electronic tools all make some reasonable process choices much harder.

Timeboxing: Events, Ceremonies, and Cycles each end when the time is up. Although the timing in our story coincides, in real life the sprint ends after a set amount of time, even if the story is unfinished. The standup is bounded at one minute per person, not when the person is done talking. Other events also end when time finishes, not based on completeness.

Made in the USA
Middletown, DE
08 July 2021

43819534R00031